DAVID
LANCE
GOINES
POSTERS

Editor's note: The Goines numbers at the end of each caption are Goines' own chronological reference numbers. Two redundant images are not illustrated: Goines 15 is an earlier draft of Goines 85, and Goines 22 is an alternate version of Goines 21. So that we only had to run gold ink on one side of each sheet, a few images are slightly out of sequence.

Foreword by Charles Shere

The qualities which inform David Goines' work—dedication, patience, a sense of line, avoidance of irrelevancies, attentiveness to detail—inform much of his life as well, and derive from it. The eldest of eight children, he was born in 1945 of parents who cheerfully pursue lives of total preoccupation. Goines inherits his eye from his mother, who paints, weaves, sculpts, and views with interest and devotion, and his analytical mind from his father, a hydraulic engineer with a love for clarity, logic, and culture as well as argument.

His tastes, interests and values are all one, and all determined by a concern for correctness, for propriety. This concern amounts almost to a compulsion. Directed toward others, it is tempered by tolerance and a sense of humor—as long as his own work is not interfered with. Directed inward, it is apparent in a notable single-mindedness which does not allow for distractions. The energy directed toward self-taught calligraphy while still in public school, toward Latin in college, toward the sustained and intensive study of Carolingian and then Renaissance calligraphy, of Irish illumination, of the proper geometric ratios of margins and text bodies, of the construction of the Roman capitals—this is a single energy, characterized best in my memory of David sitting at his desk, compass in hand, using a large number of closely related circles to define the correct proportions of a capital letter which had the look of freehand grace and spontaneity.

Of the many influences on his work the most important is that of his press, for David has always done his own presswork, confirming and developing in actual printing the concepts of the drafting table. His color sense, for example, is a direct outgrowth of fascination with the varieties and the subtleties of the possible. The calligrapher's sense of line combines with the offset lithographer's awareness of tone and tonal balance, resulting in work which uses the medium sensibly and directly. He devotes himself to continued investigation of the intrinsic possibilities of the medium itself, in process as well as concept, and so continues to expand his own potential.

A Conversation with David Lance Goines

Tell me something about your education and other influences on your work. How did you start doing posters?

Aside from that level of education required by law, lacking which, one's parents will be tossed in the slammer, I have but one year of higher education, wrested from the complaining body of the University of California at Berkeley. Due to a serious difference of opinion concerning the validity of the First Amendment of the U.S. Constitution, I was given an opportunity to seek gainful employment somewhat sooner than I had intended, and was taken on as an apprentice pressman in early 1965 at the Berkeley Free Press, where I printed damned near every piece of inflammatory trash for damned near every radical cause for damned near seven years. At the end of that time, I was tired of radical causes, being tossed in the clink, and eating cold beans out of a can. The Berkeley Free Press metamorphosed into the butterfly of Saint Heironymous Press, and began printing books, wedding announcements and posters. Posters became the main draw, and replaced the other kinds of design work. I learned to do by doing, and crammed in whatever education I could along the way. So far the lack of formal education has not proved an impediment. Indeed, I can't think of how one would go about learning a trade and going to college at the same time. The two seem, to some extent, mutually exclusive.

The influences on my artistic career are not much different from those that have influenced anyone else's career in the graphic arts. Probably the biggest difference is that I print all my own stuff.

I have consciously emulated the work of those artists whom I admire, most notably Ludwig Hohlwein, Charles Rennie Mackintosh, Hans Rudi Erdt, Albrecht Durer, Hokusai and Hiroshige. My mother received a Master's Degree in Fine Art from the University of Wisconsin. Much of what I apply as basic rules comes directly from her, and it is certainly the case that her skills and interests in calligraphy and lettering were of great importance in my early graphic arts career. My father is a civil engineer, and there is no question but that he also had a strong influence on my ideas of good design. The beauty of a dam or bridge is a result of the skill and logic with which it is designed and built. My book **A Constructed Roman Alphabet** represents, I think, a perfect synthesis of parental influences.

To some extent posters carry the stigma of being commercial art as opposed to fine art. Would you care to comment on this?

The first thing that comes to mind is the major difference between who the fine artist must please, and who the commercial artist must please. Most people work today so that they can work tomorrow, and their work is very important to them and defines them almost completely. We have two kinds of workers here whose work is superficially similar, and who the general public keeps confusing with one another, to the detriment of both. The fine artist must please only himself and one other person, that is, the buyer of the already completed work of art. All that he needs is a place to display the finished work, which has been done on spec, as it were, waiting for one sympathetic soul. The commercial artist has more restrictions put on him, and must please himself, the client and the Great God Public, or he's out of business. The work is commissioned in advance, and, before production, must be approved by the non-artist for (often) completely non-artistic reasons. The actual production of the piece is almost never done by the designer. In some areas, the artist exerts considerable control, subject, of course, to the limitations imposed by the client and the budget. Finally, the work is seen by the public, who are the real target. The work itself is usually only a vehicle for yet another work, namely the product or service advertised. Although the commercial artist's work may come to be accepted as a thing of interest in its own right, its initial purpose is subservient to something else.

Generally speaking, the commercial artist has a whole lot of other people's money, hopes, dreams and aspirations riding on his efforts, and can under no circumstances produce any "art for art's sake," or he will quickly find himself out in the street, where he can do all the fine art he wants.

Last, there is no indication of actual talent and skill when a person calls himself a "fine artist." I, for example, shun the word like the plague. I call myself a "printer," a "graphic designer," or a "graphic artist." If you call yourself an artist, who's to say if you are one or not? It's a word nearly without meaning. If I call myself a plumber, or an electrician, or a printer, it can be determined with absolute certainty in about two minutes whether I am what I say or not. These are actual skills that take years to acquire, and there's no trickery or "eye of the beholder" stuff about it. That I am a journeyman printer is not a matter of opinion, nor is it subject to fashion or whim. The same is true of my status as graphic artist. A commercial artist is in the class of skilled laborer (although most designers and commercial artists no doubt think of themselves as white collar workers, and wear neckties). If he is just beginning, he gets humble jobs commensurate with his limited abilities. Someone like Milton Glaser is very highly skilled, and the measure of that is in the effectiveness, rapidity, cleverness and economy with which he executes a client's task. Fine art is not like that. The degree of technical competence is not a measure of success or worth. There is some other matter, some connection with the Zeitgeist, which determines the popularity or insignificance of a fine artist. Skilled laborers are not "discovered" years after their death; they receive the rewards of their efforts right here on earth. Critics do not interfere with us (very much), and we make no particular effort to court them. This is changing a bit, but the skill part of it will inevitably remain, because, unlike the world of fine art, in the world of commercial art, we are talking about **real money.**

To what extent do your posters represent your own views and concerns?

Well, of course they do. How could they **not** represent everything I am? I suppose what you mean to ask is "To what extent do you use your posters as a forum for your own views and opinions, and as a persuader of others to share or act upon those views and opinions?"

I am just about as non-political as you can get, in that I hate, fear and mistrust all political groups and politicians as evil, dangerous and dishonest, having no power to do good, and great power to do harm. This is an opinion I held when I was young for no reason other than instinct, and which I now hold for very good reasons based on a wealth of experience. My second poster, "Qui Tacet Consentit" represents the last gasp of my overt political persona, and not a very strident gasp, at that. My forty-sixth poster, for my friend Harry Weininger, is in a manner of speaking an advertisement for his attempt at the elective office of Berkeley City Council. He was not elected. That's it for posters that could be called political. I suppose that the near absence of such posters must constitute a rather strong statement in itself, times being what they are.

I will not do any work for any organization which is overtly of a political nature. Furthermore, I will not work through an intermediary (such as an interior decorator or an advertising agency), and will deal with a client only on a one-to-one basis. If I feel that I cannot whole-heartedly sympathize with the client's product or service, then I don't work for him. I prefer to work for local clients, as I feel that I will do a better job for someone who looks at the world the same way I do, and for an audience of people who are somewhat the same as me and the client. I probably will work increasingly for faraway clients, but will continue to apply these standards as best I can.

I have two clients, Chez Panisse and The Pacific Film Archive, for whom I have done fifteen and twenty-five posters, respectively. Perhaps these posters provide an insight into my views and concerns. From each of these clients, I have an open commission, and can do whatever I want to do whenever I want to do it. This completely-free hand must necessarily show, in the selection of images and subjects, what ideas I have and wish to express.

Some posters are issued as unlimited editions, while others are signed and numbered. What is your own practice, and what are the determining factors in your choice?

All things, despite what the Franklin Mint would lead you to believe, are of necessity limited. There always comes a point when you have to stop doing one thing and go on to the next. I print the number of posters requested by the client, plus a comfortable margin for disaster, plus about five hundred for my own use. After the first printing, the thrill is gone, and I rarely reprint. Of the posters printed, I sign three hundred twenty-six: three hundred numbered 1-300, and twenty-six lettered A-Z as artist's proofs. The numbered ones go to the Thackrey & Robertson Gallery, and the lettered ones are for my own purposes. I also sign three sets of progressives, which are the posters with the colors on them in sequence of printing. One set of these goes to the client, and the rest go to Thackrey & Robertson. The client gets what he ordered (plus or minus 10% as per trade practice).

What printing methods and materials do you use, and why? What is your role in the printing?

The posters are printed by photo-offset lithography, on an ATF Solna Chief 24, serial #824, manufactured in 1954 and completely paid for. I print on Mohawk Superfine 80# Cover, white and soft white, depending on what seems right for the specific job. I have used other sheets in the past, such as Strathmore, but the Mohawk is the best uncoated sheet I have ever run. There just aren't many sheets that run well and can take the punishment of being put through an offset press twenty-six times. Good paper does just what it's supposed to, leaving the pressman free to make decisions about the image. Bad paper can make life pure hell. Automatic machinery requires a high order of uniformity and predictability from a sheet, so I have no use for handmade or moldmade papers.

I am by trade a journeyman printer, and do all the production on my posters myself. This is the biggest limiting factor, as large quantities (more than 5000) are completely beyond me, and special requirements, such as coated sheets, are not what I do.

The printing is solid-color lithography, as opposed to four-color process, and a given poster may run as high as nineteen colors and twenty-two passes, although ten to twelve is more common. Some run as few as one to five colors, but my evil genius rarely allows such simplicity. I mix all the colors myself, according to a relatively simple scheme of complementary tertiary pastels. I do not use the PMS or any similar color system.

I don't have a press capable of doing gold foil stamping, so that part is done by Marier Engraving in San Francisco.

The color separations are photo-mechanical, from key-line art. The original artwork is black key-line on white Strathmore Artist's Drawing, two ply. The original artwork is almost always about one-fourth the size of the finished poster. I Xerox the original art, and color the copy with watercolors or gouache, to work out the color scheme and give me something to show the client.

What are the pros and cons of being a poster artist?

Being a poster artist exclusively is a bit like putting all your eggs in one basket. I can concentrate intensely on the task of designing and printing posters, and get really good at it, but this high profile single crop has the hazard of becoming fashionable, and of course, unfashionable. Also, as I do all my own production, and refuse to make my tasks easier by dealing with advertising agencies and other such middlemen, I have a severely limited production, which is just about enough to keep me one jump ahead of the sheriff. I always mean to do more, or charge more, or something, but I never seem to get much more done this year than the last, no matter how I try.

From what I can tell, there seems to be a fathomless demand for design work of all kinds, and a great demand for posters. Why this should be, I cannot say.

How are your posters marketed?

The client, having gotten what he ordered, disposes of the posters as he sees fit. As things that are given away free are little valued, some modest charge is usually made to those who want the poster. Often, the client is able to recoup the costs of his poster by this means.

Sometimes the client will sell a small number of the posters to various dealers and framing shops, which in turn merchandise the poster over a wider geographical area. Most of the posters, however, are sold by the client from his own location, thereby increasing their value as advertising: in order to get the poster, people must find out where the client is, go there, look around, and generally do all the things that ads are supposed to get people to do.

The signed posters, which, except for the signature, are identical in all respects to the posters that go to the client, go to my exclusive representative, Thackrey & Robertson Gallery. They, in turn, distribute the posters to various galleries about the United States, and retail posters directly from their own gallery. They have represented me since 1972, and this relationship is beginning to look permanent.

In response to some evidence of piracy, I have licensed Portal Publications to reproduce, by four-color process, a certain number of posters that they feel have a broad market appeal. These reprints are sold in many inexpensive poster outlets in this land and overseas.

I do not sell either the originals or the reprints myself, as it is more trouble than it is worth.

Where do posters fit into your long-term artistic goals?

I will continue doing posters as long as a market for my work exists, which I fervently hope will be a long time. I am interested in three-dimensional design and industrial design, and have done a few projects in that direction. I am also interested in teaching, and do a bit of that every year. I enjoy writing, and now that I finally have a good word processor, I am writing quite a bit. I might even depart from technical writing into fiction, but don't hold your breath. It's possible that one of these will become more important, or that some new and unsuspected thing will arise, rendering all my speculations foolish.

What, for you, is the hardest part of making a poster?

The most difficult part of poster design for me is simply coming up with an idea. Once I have that, I'm on rails. A poster takes me, all told, about two hundred hours, a good half of which is invisible thinking. I know that if I just beat my head against the wall long enough, an idea will infallibly result, but there is always the nameless terror that maybe **this** time the Muse is not merely hitchhiking through Georgia but has been kidnapped, murdered and tumbled into a ditch. Or maybe she's mad at me.

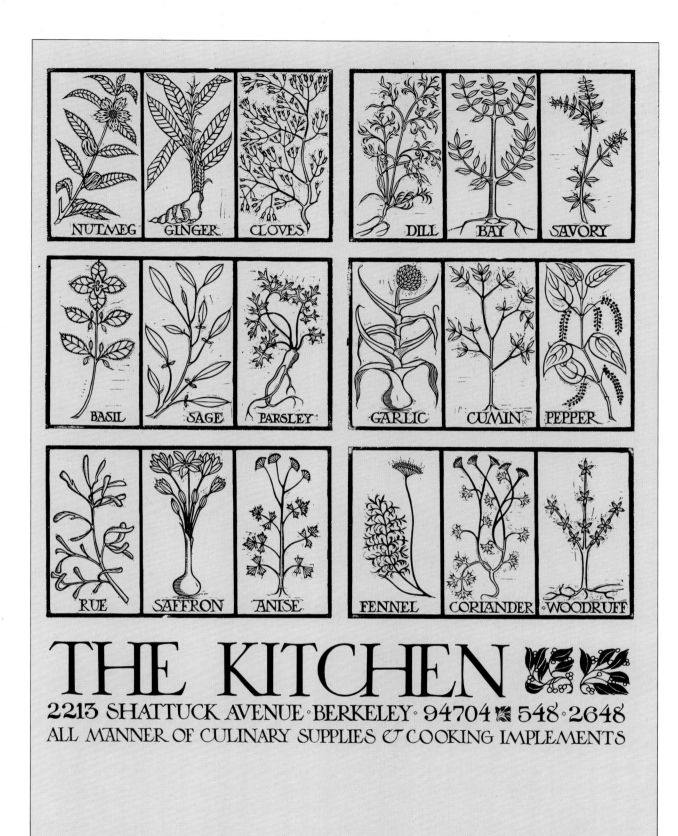

THE KITCHEN

2213 SHATTUCK AVENUE · BERKELEY · 94704 ☙ 548·2648
ALL MANNER OF CULINARY SUPPLIES & COOKING IMPLEMENTS

THE KITCHEN, 1968, ONE COLOR, 18 x 24″, GOINES 1

QUI TACET CONSENTIT

Berkeley Graphic Arts::Lithographers::1705 Grove Street::Berkeley::California 94709::USA::(415) 549-1405

QUI TACET CONSENTIT, 1969, TWO COLORS, 17½ x 22½", GOINES 2

JAMES MICHAEL BENNETT AND SWEET KATHERINE ANN REDDY ARE TO BE MARRIED AT ST. MARK'S CHURCH 2314 BANCROFT WAY BERKELEY CALIFORNIA ON SATURDAY NOVEMBER 29 AT 2:00 PM::A RECEPTION IS TO FOLLOW IMMEDIATELY::RSVP 283-2749::841-1045:: ::

BENNETT WEDDING ANNOUNCEMENT, 1969, ONE COLOR, 17½ x 22½", GOINES 3

VELO-SPORT BICYCLES, 1970, FIVE COLORS, 18 x 24″, GOINES 4

THE SAN FRANCISCO MIME TROUPE, 1970, THREE COLORS, 17½ x 24″, GOINES 5

WOODWORK
KIP MESIROW:: ::RON HERMAN
NEWMAN GALLERY::COLLEGE & DWIGHT::BERKELEY::MAY 1970

WOODWORK, 1970, TWO COLORS, 18 x 24", GOINES 6

The law,
in its majestic equality,
forbids the rich
as well as the poor
to sleep under bridges,
to beg in the streets,
& to steal bread.

Anatole France

MICHAEL KELLEY IS PLEASED TO ANNOUNCE TO HIS FRIENDS & CLIENTS HIS ASSOCIATION WITH THE FIRM OF FRANCK, HILL, STENDER, ZIEGLER & HENDON, ATTORNEYS AT LAW. HIS PRACTICE WILL BE CONDUCTED FROM THEIR OFFICES AT 2905 TELEGRAPH AVENUE, BERKELEY 94705. (415) 845-4123

ANATOLE FRANCE QUOTE, 1970, ONE COLOR, 15 x 24", GOINES 7

RAINBOW ZENITH, 1970, EIGHT COLORS ON SILVER PAPER, 17½ x 22½'', GOINES 8

FOTO-GRAPHIX, 1971, THREE COLORS, 17 x 24", GOINES 9

On the 10th of April, 1971, Harold Tim Hoffman & Lisa Goines were married. To share their joy & pleasure, they invite you to attend a reception on Saturday, April 17th, 1971, at the home of George Berns, 6615 Dana, Oakland.

HOFFMAN WEDDING ANNOUNCEMENT, 1971, THREE COLORS, 17½ x 22½″, GOINES 10

BERKELEY ARTS CALENDAR, *1971, FOUR COLORS, 18 x 24'', GOINES 11*

POETRY READING

YIDDISH & HEBREW POETRY READING & CONVERSATION
YEHUDA AMICHAI, CHANA FAERSTEIN BLOCH, ROBERT ALTER
BYRNE NEWHART, ORIGINAL COMPOSITION
SATURDAY NIGHT AT 8:30   DECEMBER 18, 1971
2736 BANCROFT WAY, BERKELEY
TICKETS 525-0731 & 535-1013 $3, STUDENTS $2

POETRY READING, 1971, TWO COLORS, 15 x 24", GOINES 12

VD - DON'T GIVE THE GIFT THAT GOES ON GIVING VD

Berkeley VD Clinic 830 University Avenue
Telephone : 845-0197
Drop-in hours: Monday: 1:30-5:30
⠀⠀⠀⠀⠀⠀⠀⠀⠀⠀⠀**Wednesday: 4-6**
⠀⠀⠀⠀⠀⠀⠀⠀⠀⠀⠀**Friday: 8:30am-10:30am**

BERKELEY VD CLINIC, 1971, FOUR COLORS, 18 x 24'', GOINES 13

CHEZ PANISSE, 1972, FOUR COLORS, 15 x 24'', GOINES 14

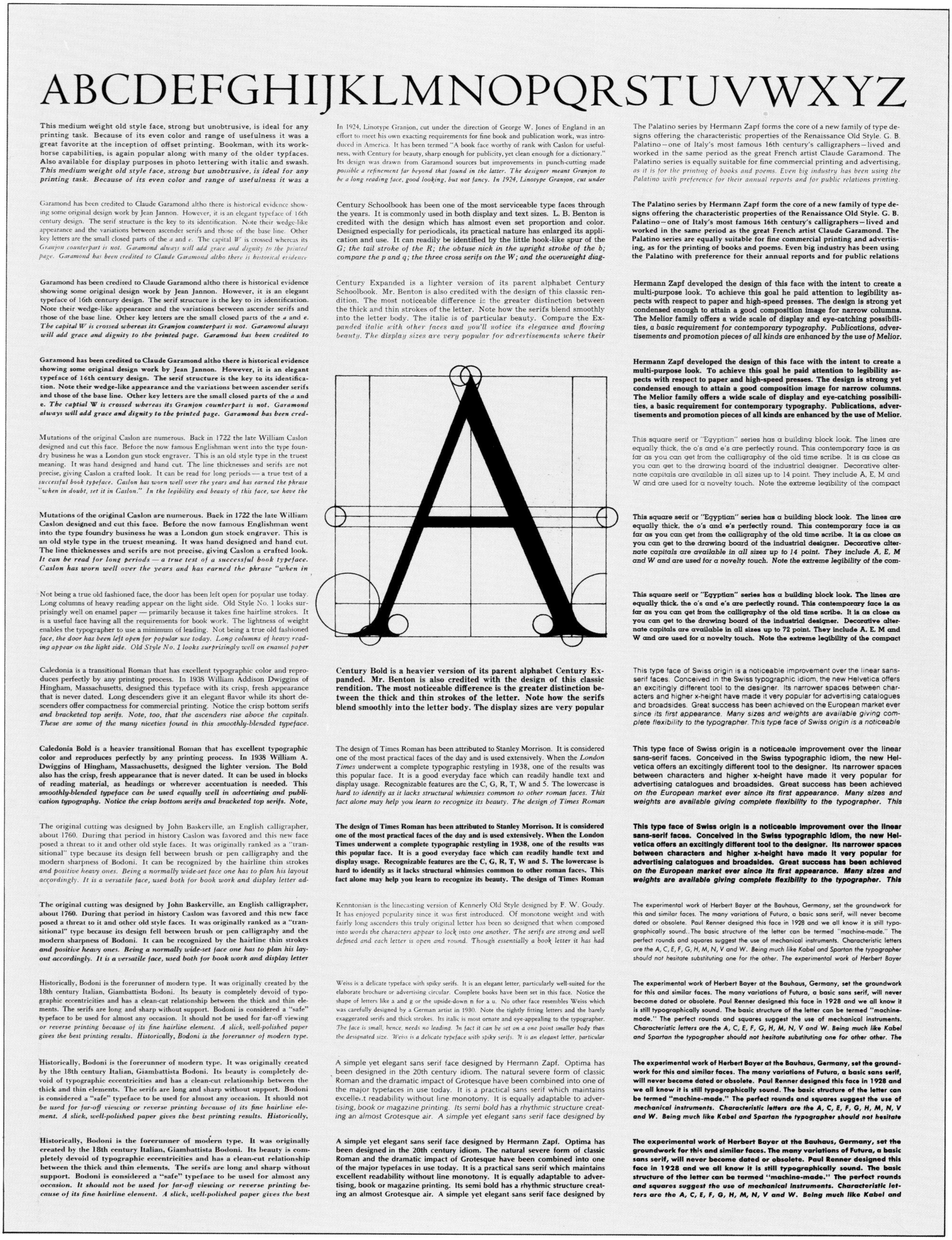

ABCDEFGHIJKLMNOPQRSTUVWXYZ

This medium weight old style face, strong but unobtrusive, is ideal for any printing task. Because of its even color and range of usefulness it was a great favorite at the inception of offset printing. Bookman, with its work-horse capabilities, is again popular along with many of the older typfaces. Also available for display purposes in photo lettering with italic and swash. *This medium weight old style face, strong but unobtrusive, is ideal for any printing task. Because of its even color and range of usefulness it was a*

Garamond has been credited to Claude Garamond altho there is historical evidence showing some original design work by Jean Jannon. However, it is an elegant typeface of 16th century design. The serif structure is the key to its identification. Note their wedge-like appearance and the variations between ascender serifs and those of the base line. Other key letters are the small closed parts of the *a* and *e*. The capital *W* is crossed whereas its *Granjon counterpart is not. Garamond always will add grace and dignity to the printed page. Garamond has been credited to Claude Garamond altho there is historical evidence*

Garamond has been credited to Claude Garamond altho there is historical evidence showing some original design work by Jean Jannon. However, it is an elegant typeface of 16th century design. The serif structure is the key to its identification. Note their wedge-like appearance and the variations between ascender serifs and those of the base line. Other key letters are the small closed parts of the *a* and *e*. *The capital W is crossed whereas its Granjon counterpart is not. Garamond always will add grace and dignity to the printed page. Garamond has been credited to*

Garamond has been credited to Claude Garamond altho there is historical evidence showing some original design work by Jean Jannon. However, it is an elegant typeface of 16th century design. The serif structure is the key to its identification. Note their wedge-like appearance and the variations between ascender serifs and those of the base line. Other key letters are the small closed parts of the *a* and *e*. *The captial W is crossed whereas its Granjon counterpart is not. Garamond always will add grace and dignity to the printed page. Garamond has been cred-*

Mutations of the original Caslon are numerous. Back in 1722 the late William Caslon designed and cut this face. Before the now famous Englishman went into the type foundry business he was a London gun stock engraver. This is an old style type in the truest meaning. It was hand designed and hand cut. The line thicknesses and serifs are not precise, giving Caslon a crafted look. It can be read for long periods — a true test of a *successful book typeface. Caslon has worn well over the years and has earned the phrase "when in doubt, set it in Caslon." In the legibility and beauty of this face, we have the*

Mutations of the original Caslon are numerous. Back in 1722 the late William Caslon designed and cut this face. Before the now famous Englishman went into the type foundry business he was a London gun stock engraver. This is an old style type in the truest meaning. It was hand designed and hand cut. The line thicknesses and serifs are not precise, giving Caslon a crafted look. *It can be read for long periods — a true test of a successful book typeface. Caslon has worn well over the years and has earned the phrase "when in*

Not being a true old fashioned face, the door has been left open for popular use today. Long columns of heavy reading appear on the light side. Old Style No. 1 looks surprisingly well on enamel paper — primarily because it takes fine hairline strokes. It is a useful face having all the requirements for book work. The lightness of weight enables the typographer to use a minimum of leading. Not being a true old fashioned *face, the door has been left open for popular use today. Long columns of heavy reading appear on the light side. Old Style No. 1 looks surprisingly well on enamel paper*

Caledonia is a transitional Roman that has excellent typographic color and reproduces perfectly by any printing process. In 1938 William Addison Dwiggins of Hingham, Massachusetts, designed this typeface with its crisp, fresh appearance that is never dated. Long descenders give it an elegant flavor while its short descenders offer compactness for commercial printing. Notice the crisp bottom serifs *and bracketed top serifs. Note, too, that the ascenders rise above the capitals. These are some of the many niceties found in this smoothly-blended typeface.*

Caledonia Bold is a heavier transitional Roman that has excellent typographic color and reproduces perfectly by any printing process. In 1938 William A. Dwiggins of Hingham, Massachusetts, designed the lighter version. The Bold also has the crisp, fresh appearance that is never dated. It can be used in blocks of reading material, as headings or wherever accentuation is needed. This *smoothly-blended typeface can be used equally well in advertising and publication typography. Notice the crisp bottom serifs and bracketed top serifs. Note,*

The original cutting was designed by John Baskerville, an English calligrapher, about 1760. During that period in history Caslon was favored and this new face posed a threat to it and other old style faces. It was originally ranked as a "transitional" type because its design fell between brush or pen calligraphy and the modern sharpness of Bodoni. It can be recognized by the hairline thin strokes *and positive heavy ones. Being a normally wide-set face one has to plan his layout accordingly. It is a versatile face, used both for book work and display letter ad-*

The original cutting was designed by John Baskerville, an English calligrapher, about 1760. During that period in history Caslon was favored and this new face posed a threat to it and other old style faces. It was originally ranked as a "transitional" type because its design fell between brush or pen calligraphy and the modern sharpness of Bodoni. It can be recognized by the hairline thin strokes *and positive heavy ones. Being a normally wide-set face one has to plan his layout accordingly. It is a versatile face, used both for book work and display letter*

Historically, Bodoni is the forerunner of modern type. It was originally created by the 18th century Italian, Giambattista Bodoni. Its beauty is completely devoid of typographic eccentricities and has a clean-cut relationship between the thick and thin elements. The serifs are long and sharp without support. Bodoni is considered a "safe" typeface to be used for almost any occasion. It should not be used for far-off viewing *or reverse printing because of its fine hairline element. A slick, well-polished paper gives the best printing results. Historically, Bodoni is the forerunner of modern type.*

Historically, Bodoni is the forerunner of modern type. It was originally created by the 18th century Italian, Giambattista Bodoni. Its beauty is completely devoid of typographic eccentricities and has a clean-cut relationship between the thick and thin elements. The serifs are long and sharp without support. Bodoni is considered a "safe" typeface to be used for almost any occasion. It should not *be used for far-off viewing or reverse printing because of its fine hairline element. A slick, well-polished paper gives the best printing results. Historically,*

Historically, Bodoni is the forerunner of modern type. It was originally created by the 18th century Italian, Giambattista Bodoni. Its beauty is completely devoid of typographic eccentricities and has a clean-cut relationship between the thick and thin elements. The serifs are long and sharp without support. Bodoni is considered a "safe" typeface to be used for almost any *occasion. It should not be used for far-off viewing or reverse printing because of its fine hairline element. A slick, well-polished paper gives the best*

In 1924, Linotype Granjon, cut under the direction of George W. Jones of England in an effort to meet his own exacting requirements for fine book and publication work, was introduced in America. It has been termed "A book face worthy of rank with Caslon for usefulness, with Century for beauty, sharp enough for publicity, yet clean enough for a dictionary." Its design was drawn from Garamond sources but improvements in punch-cutting made *possible a refinement far beyond that found in the latter. The designer meant Granjon to be a long reading face, good looking, but not fancy. In 1924, Linotype Granjon, cut under*

Century Schoolbook has been one of the most serviceable type faces through the years. It is commonly used in both display and text sizes. L. B. Benton is credited with the design which has almost even set proportion and color. Designed especially for periodicals, its practical nature has enlarged its application and use. It can readily be identified by the little hook-like spur of the *G; the tail stroke of the R; the obtuse nick in the upright stroke of the b; compare the p and q; the three cross serifs on the W; and the overweight diag-*

Century Expanded is a lighter version of its parent alphabet Century Schoolbook. Mr. Benton is also credited with the design of this classic rendition. The most noticeable difference is the greater distinction between the thick and thin strokes of the letter. Note how the serifs blend smoothly into the letter body. The italic is of particular beauty. Compare the Ex-*panded italic with other faces and you'll notice its elegance and flowing beauty. The display sizes are very popular for advertisements where their*

Century Bold is a heavier version of its parent alphabet Century Expanded. Mr. Benton is also credited with the design of this classic rendition. The most noticeable difference is the greater distinction between the thick and thin strokes of the letter. Note how the serifs blend smoothly into the letter body. The display sizes are very popular

The design of Times Roman has been attributed to Stanley Morrison. It is considered one of the most practical faces of the day and is used extensively. When the *London Times* underwent a complete typographic restyling in 1938, one of the results was this popular face. It is a good everyday face which can readily handle text and display usage. Recognizable features are the C, G, R, T, W and 5. The lowercase is *hard to identify as it lacks structural whimsies common to other roman faces. This fact alone may help you learn to recognize its beauty. The design of Times Roman*

The design of Times Roman has been attributed to Stanley Morrison. It is considered one of the most practical faces of the day and is used extensively. When the London Times underwent a complete typographic restyling in 1938, one of the results was this popular face. It is a good everyday face which can readily handle text and display usage. Recognizable features are the C, G, R, T, W and 5. The lowercase is hard to identify as it lacks structural whimsies common to other roman faces. This fact alone may help you learn to recognize its beauty. The design of Times Roman

Kenntonian is the linecasting version of Kennerly Old Style designed by F. W. Goudy. It has enjoyed popularity since it was first introduced. Of monotone weight and with fairly long ascenders this truly original letter has been so designed that when composed *into words the characters appear to lock into one another. The serifs are strong and well defined and each letter is open and round. Though essentially a book letter it has had*

Weiss is a delicate typeface with spiky serifs. It is an elegant letter, particularly well-suited for the elaborate brochure or advertising circular. Complete books have been set in this face. Notice the shape of letters like a and g or the upside-down n for a u. No other face resembles Weiss which was carefully designed by a German artist in 1930. Note the tightly fitting letters and the barely exaggerated serifs and thick strokes. Its italic is most ornate and eye-appealing to the typographer. *The face is small, hence, needs no leading. In fact it can be set on a one point smaller body than the designated size. Weiss is a delicate typeface with spiky serifs. It is an elegant letter, particular*

A simple yet elegant sans serif face designed by Hermann Zapf. Optima has been designed in the 20th century idiom. The natural severe form of classic Roman and the dramatic impact of Grotesque have been combined into one of the major typefaces in use today. It is a practical sans serif which maintains excellent readability without line monotony. It is equally adaptable to adver-*tising, book or magazine printing. Its semi bold has a rhythmic structure creating an almost Grotesque air. A simple yet elegant sans serif face designed by*

A simple yet elegant sans serif face designed by Hermann Zapf. Optima has been designed in the 20th century idiom. The natural severe form of classic Roman and the dramatic impact of Grotesque have been combined into one of the major typefaces in use today. It is a practical sans serif which maintains excellent readability without line monotony. It is equally adaptable to advertising, book or magazine printing. Its semi bold has a rhythmic structure creating an almost Grotesque air. A simple yet elegant sans serif face designed by

The Palatino series by Hermann Zapf forms the core of a new family of type designs offering the characteristic properties of the Renaissance Old Style. G. B. Palatino—one of Italy's most famous 16th century's calligraphers—lived and worked in the same period as the great French artist Claude Garamond. The Palatino series is equally suitable for fine commercial printing and advertising, *as it is for the printing of books and poems. Even big industry has been using the Palatino with preference for their annual reports and for public relations printing.*

The Palatino series by Hermann Zapf form the core of a new family of type designs offering the characteristic properties of the Renaissance Old Style. G. B. Palatino—one of Italy's most famous 16th century's calligraphers—lived and worked in the same period as the great French artist Claude Garamond. The Palatino series are equally suitable for fine commercial printing and advertising, as for the printing of books and poems. Even big industry has been using the Palatino with preference for their annual reports and for public relations

Hermann Zapf developed the design of this face with the intent to create a multi-purpose look. To achieve this goal he paid attention to legibility aspects with respect to paper and high-speed presses. The design is strong yet condensed enough to attain a good composition image for narrow columns. The Melior family offers a wide scale of display and eye-catching possibilities, *a basic requirement for contemporary typography. Publications, advertisements and promotion pieces of all kinds are enhanced by the use of Melior.*

Hermann Zapf developed the design of this face with the intent to create a multi-purpose look. To achieve this goal he paid attention to legibility aspects with respect to paper and high-speed presses. The design is strong yet condensed enough to attain a good composition image for narrow columns. The Melior family offers a wide scale of display and eye-catching possibilities, a basic requirement for contemporary typography. Publications, advertisements and promotion pieces of all kinds are enhanced by the use of Melior.

This square serif or "Egyptian" series has a building block look. The lines are equally thick, the o's and e's are perfectly round. This contemporary face is as far as you can get from the calligraphy of the old time scribe. It is as close as you can get to the drawing board of the industrial designer. Decorative alternate capitals are available in all sizes up to 14 point. They include A, E, M and W and are used for a novelty touch. Note the extreme legibility of the compact

This square serif or "Egyptian" series has a building block look. The lines are equally thick, the o's and e's perfectly round. This contemporary face is as far as you can get from the calligraphy of the old time scribe. It is as close as you can get to the drawing board of the industrial designer. Decorative alter-*nate capitals are available in all sizes up to 14 point. They include A, E, M and W and are used for a novelty touch. Note the extreme legibility of the com-*

This square serif or "Egyptian" series has a building block look. The lines are equally thick, the o's and e's are perfectly round. This contemporary face is as far as you can get from the calligraphy of the old time scribe. It is as close as you can get to the drawing board of the industrial designer. Decorative alternate capitals are available in all sizes up to 72 point. They include A, E, M and W and are used for a novelty touch. Note the extreme legibility of the compact

This type face of Swiss origin is a noticeable improvement over the linear sans-serif faces. Conceived in the Swiss typographic idiom, the new Helvetica offers an excitingly different tool to the designer. Its narrower spaces between characters and higher x-height have made it very popular for advertising catalogues and broadsides. Great success has been achieved on the European market ever *since its first appearance. Many sizes and weights are available giving complete flexibility to the typographer.* This type face of Swiss origin is a noticeable

This type face of Swiss origin is a noticeable improvement over the linear sans-serif faces. Conceived in the Swiss typographic idiom, the new Helvetica offers an excitingly different tool to the designer. Its narrower spaces between characters and higher x-height have made it very popular for advertising catalogues and broadsides. Great success has been achieved *on the European market ever since its first appearance. Many sizes and weights are available giving complete flexibility to the typographer. This*

This type face of Swiss origin is a noticeable improvement over the linear sans-serif faces. Conceived in the Swiss typographic idiom, the new Helvetica offers an excitingly different tool to the designer. Its narrower spaces between characters and higher x-height have made it very popular for advertising calatogues and broadsides. Great success has been achieved *on the European market ever since its first appearance. Many sizes and weights are available giving complete flexibility to the typographer. This*

The experimental work of Herbert Bayer at the Bauhaus, Germany, set the groundwork for this and similar faces. The many variations of Futura, a basic sans serif, will never become dated or obsolete. Paul Renner designed this face in 1928 and we all know it is still typographically sound. The basic structure of the letter can be termed "machine-made." The perfect rounds and squares suggest the use of mechanical instruments. Characteristic letters *are the A, C, E, F, G, H, M, N, V and W. Being much like Kabel and Spartan the typographer should not hesitate substituting one for the other. The experimental work of Herbert Bayer*

The experimental work of Herbert Bayer at the Bauhaus, Germany, set the groundwork for this and similar faces. The many variations of Futura, a basic sans serif, will never become dated or obsolete. Paul Renner designed this face in 1928 and we all know it is still typographically sound. The basic structure of the letter can be termed "machine-made." The perfect rounds and squares suggest the use of mechanical instruments. *Characteristic letters are the A, C, E, F, G, H, M, N, V and W. Being much like Kabel and Spartan the typographer should not hesitate substituting one for other other. The*

The experimental work of Herbert Bayer at the Bauhaus, Germany, set the groundwork for this and similar faces. The many variations of Futura, a basic sans serif, will never become dated or obsolete. Paul Renner designed this face in 1928 and we all know it is still typographically sound. The basic structure of the letter can be termed "machine-made." The perfect rounds and squares suggest the use of *mechanical instruments. Characteristic letters are the A, C, E, F, G, H, M, N, V and W. Being much like Kabel and Spartan the typographer should not hesitate*

The experimental work of Herbert Bayer at the Bauhaus, Germany, set the groundwork for this and similar faces. The many variations of Futura, a basic sans serif, will never become dated or obsolete. Paul Renner designed this face in 1928 and we all know it is still typographically sound. The basic structure of the letter can be termed "machine-made." The perfect rounds *and squares suggest the use of mechanical instruments. Characteristic letters are the A, C, E, F, G, H, M, N, V and W. Being much like Kabel and*

TYPE SPECIMEN, 1972, ONE COLOR, 18 x 24", GOINES 16

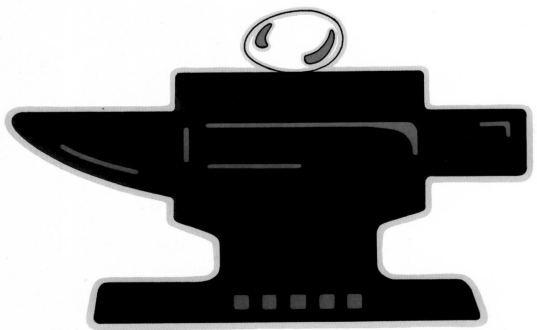

DER BLAUE ENGEL

MARLENE DIETRICH :: EMIL JANNINGS :: 1930:
DIRECTED BY : JOSEF VON STERNBERG :: UFA :

PACIFIC FILM ARCHIVE :: UC ART MUSEUM :: BERKELEY :: 2625 DURANT
TUESDAY : AUGUST 8 : 7⁰⁰ & 10³⁰ :: ALSO SHOWING—MOROCCO : AT 8⁴⁵

DER BLAUE ENGEL, 1972, FOUR COLORS, 16¾ x 24″, GOINES 17

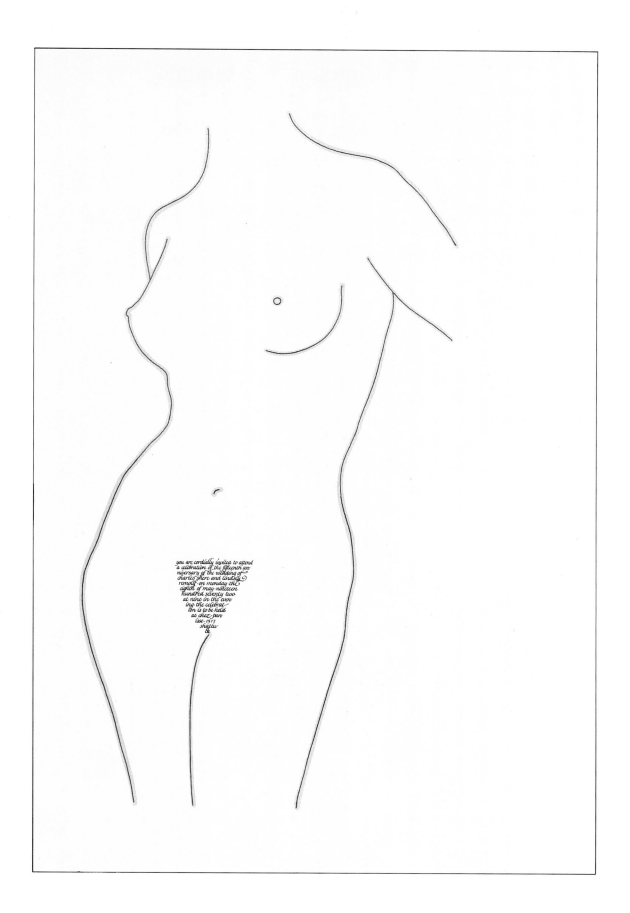

you are cordially invited to attend
a celebration of the fifteenth an~
niversary of the wedding of
charles shere and lindsey
remolif on monday the
eighth of may nineteen
hundred seventy two
at nine in the even~
ing the celebrat~
ion is to be held
at chez pan~
isse 1517
shattu~
ck

SHERE ANNIVERSARY INVITATION, 1972, TWO COLORS, 16 x 24'', GOINES 18

THE GENERAL
BUSTER KEATON ::1926::

PACIFIC FILM ARCHIVE::2625 DURANT::BERKELEY::TELEPHONE:642-1413
THE GENERAL::SHOWING SATURDAY, AUGUST 19, AT 4:30 & 7:30,ALSO,COPS

THE GENERAL, 1972, FIVE COLORS, 18 x 24'', GOINES 19

RUGGLES OF RED GAP, 1972, THREE COLORS, 18 x 24", GOINES 20

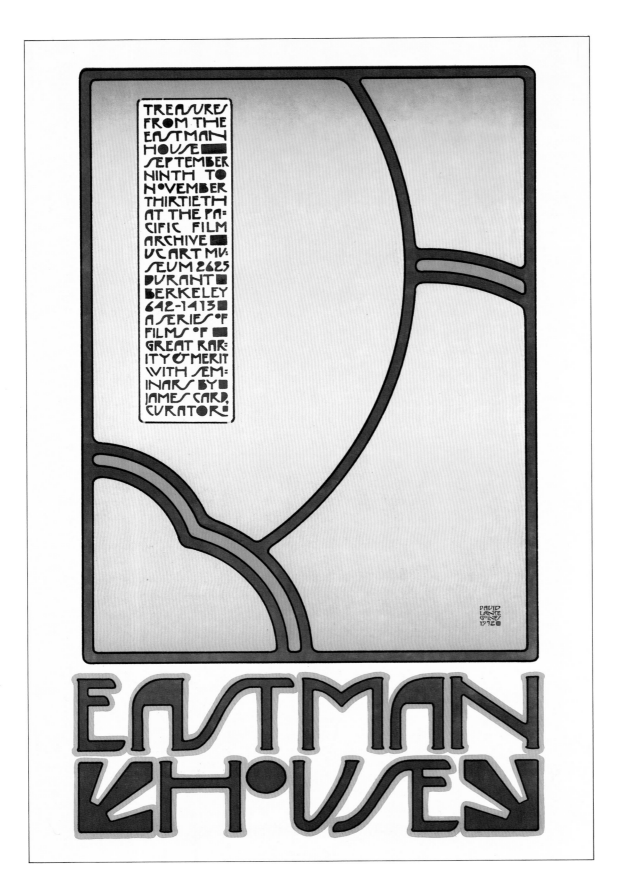

EASTMAN HOUSE, 1972, FOUR COLORS, 15½ x 24", GOINES 21

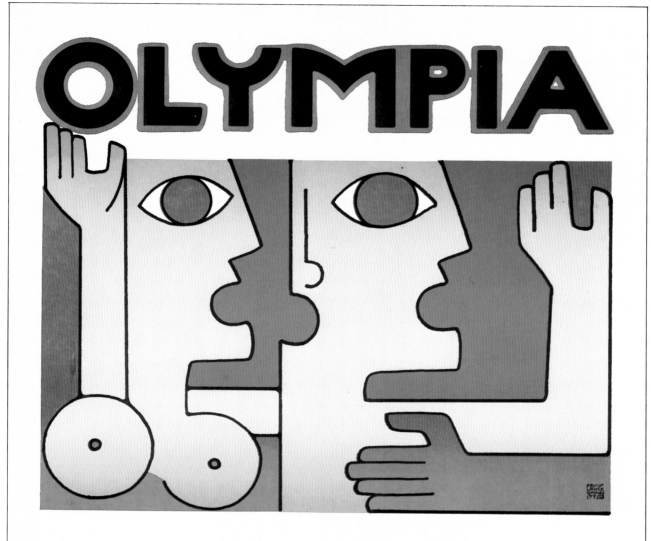

OLYMPIA

LENI RIEFENSTAHL:1936-1938
PART I:FESTIVAL OF THE NATIONS
FRIDAY:SEPTEMBER 22:AT9:3°
PART II:FESTIVAL OF BEAUTY:
SATURDAY:SEPTEMBER 23:9:3°
PARTS I AND II:SATURDAY:3:∞
PACIFIC FILM ARCHIVE:UC ART MUSEUM:2625 DURANT::

OLYMPIA, 1972, FOUR COLORS, 18 x 24″, GOINES 23

GUINNESS, 1973, SEVEN COLORS, 18 x 24'', GOINES 25

BACH, 1973, FIVE COLORS, 18 x 24'', GOINES 26

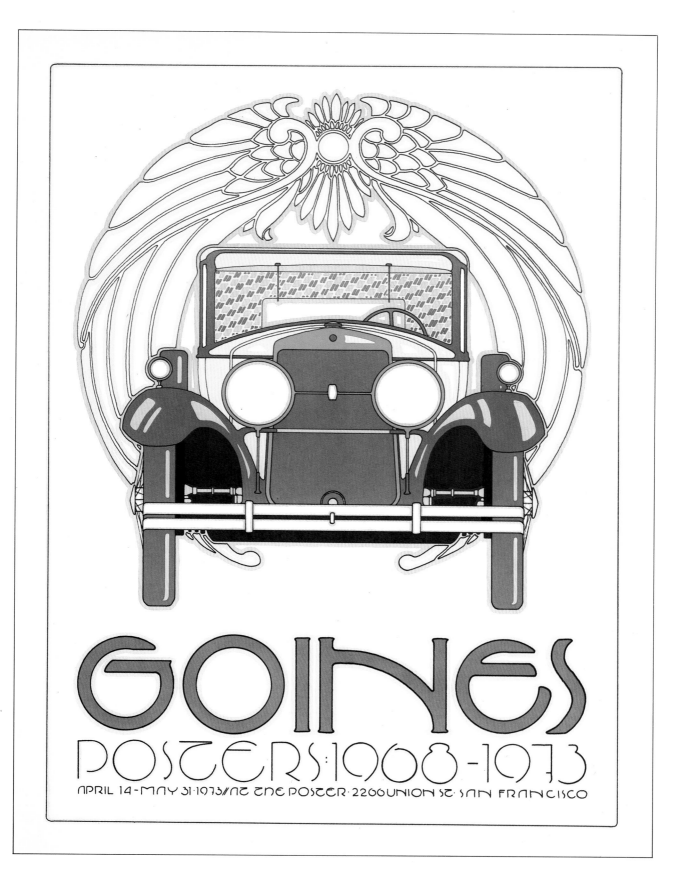

GOINES POSTERS: 1968–1973, 1973, EIGHT COLORS, 18 x 24", GOINES 27

MARIUS, 1973, FIVE COLORS, 13½ x 24″, GOINES 28

FANNY, 1973, FIVE COLORS, 13½ x 24", GOINES 29

CÉSAR, 1973, FIVE COLORS, 13½ x 24″, GOINES 30

CHEZ PANISSE
SECOND BIRTHDAY
CELEBRATION
TUESDAY AUGUST 28
SIX PM TO MIDNIGHT
CASSOULET
½ LITRE OF WINE
& SALAD ∷ $5 25
ALSO UN FILM DE
MARCEL PAGNOL

CHEZ PANISSE SECOND BIRTHDAY, 1973, FOUR COLORS, 18 x 24'', GOINES 31

CHARCUTERIE PIG-BY-THE-TAIL
PIG-BY-THE-TAIL
FRENCH-STYLE DELICATESSEN
1512 SHATTUCK   843-4004

IMAGES·MÉDIÉVALES

TUESDAY·OCTOBER 30·7 & 9⁴⁵·AT THE PACIFIC FILM ARCHIVE·2625 DURANT·BERKELEY

IMAGES MÉDIÉVALES, 1973, NINE COLORS PLUS GOLD, 18 x 24″, GOINES 33

KARL·KARDEL·Cͦ

BUILDERS · PAINTERS · DECORATORS

4926·EAST·12ᵀᴴ·STREET·OAKLAND·CALIFORNIA·94601·SHOP:261-4150

KARL KARDEL CO., 1974, EIGHT COLORS, 18 x 24″, GOINES 34

BART AND ITS INFORMATION CENTER
OPERATE MONDAY THROUGH FRIDAY
FROM 6:00 AM TO 8:00 PM. CALL
US ABOUT BART AND LOCAL BUS
SERVICE. CHINESE AND SPANISH
SPEAKING OPERATORS ARE ON DUTY
FROM 8:00 AM TO 5:00 PM

SAN FRANCISCO/DALY CITY AREA 788-B-A-R-T
OAKLAND/BERKELEY/ORINDA AREA.465-B-A-R-T
LAFAYETTE/CONCORD AREA 933-B-A-R-T
FREMONT/UNION CITY AREA.............793-B-A-R-T
HAYWARD/SAN LEANDRO AREA.........783-B-A-R-T
RICHMOND/EL CERRITO AREA 236-B-A-R-T
LIVERMORE/PLEASANTON AREA.......462-B-A-R-T

BART, 1974, FIVE COLORS, 21 x 22'', GOINES 35

GOINES, 1974, FIVE COLORS PLUS GOLD, 13 x 24'', GOINES 37

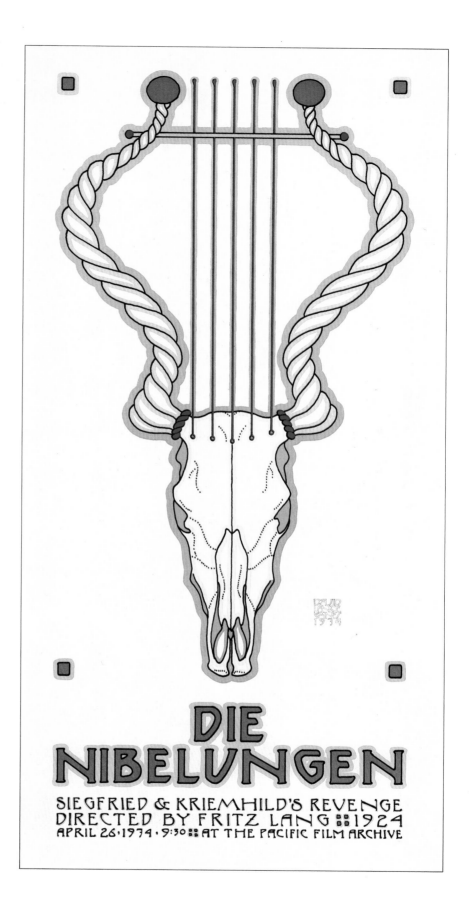

DIE NIBELUNGEN, 1974, SIX COLORS PLUS GOLD, 12 x 24″, GOINES 38

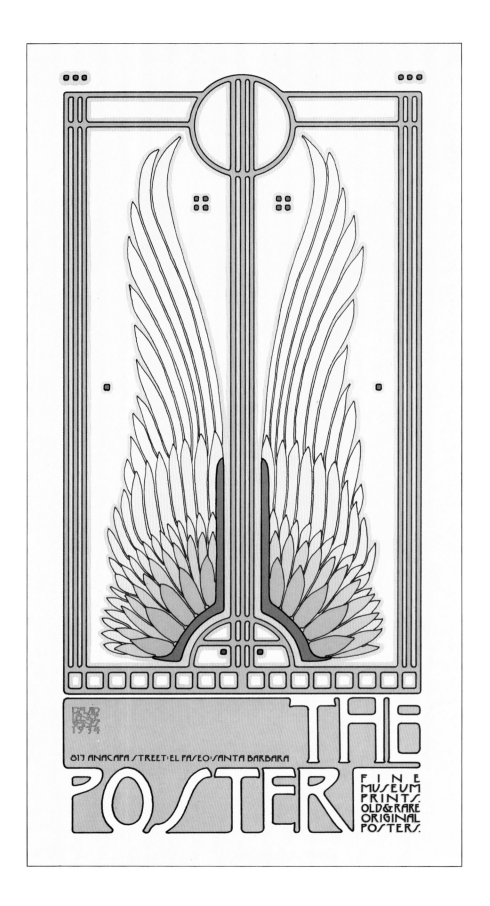

THE POSTER, 1974, NINE COLORS, 12¼ x 24", GOINES 36

LES ANIMAUX, 1974, TWO COLORS, 24 x 18'', GOINES 39

AMERICA, 1974, TWELVE COLORS, 18 x 24'', GOINES 40

CHEZ PANISSE THIRD BIRTHDAY, 1974, SIX COLORS, 18 x 24'', GOINES 41

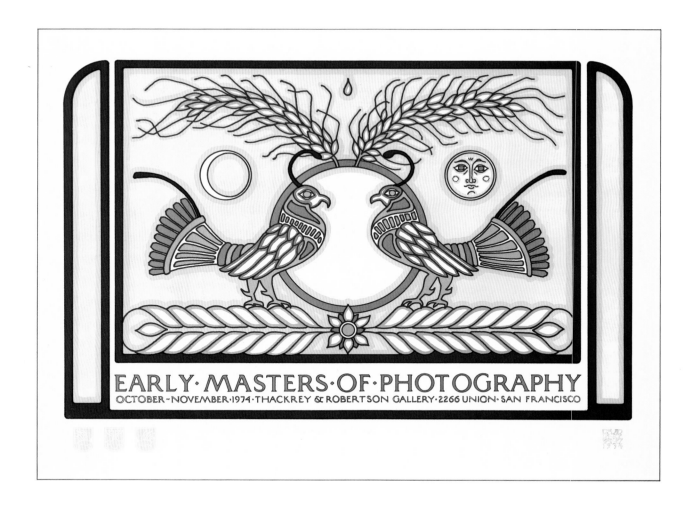

EARLY MASTERS OF PHOTOGRAPHY, 1974, SIX COLORS, 24 x 18'', GOINES 42

INDIA INK GALLERY, 1974, THREE COLORS, 16¼ x 24″, GOINES 43

BY HAND, 1974, FIVE COLORS, 18 x 24", GOINES 44

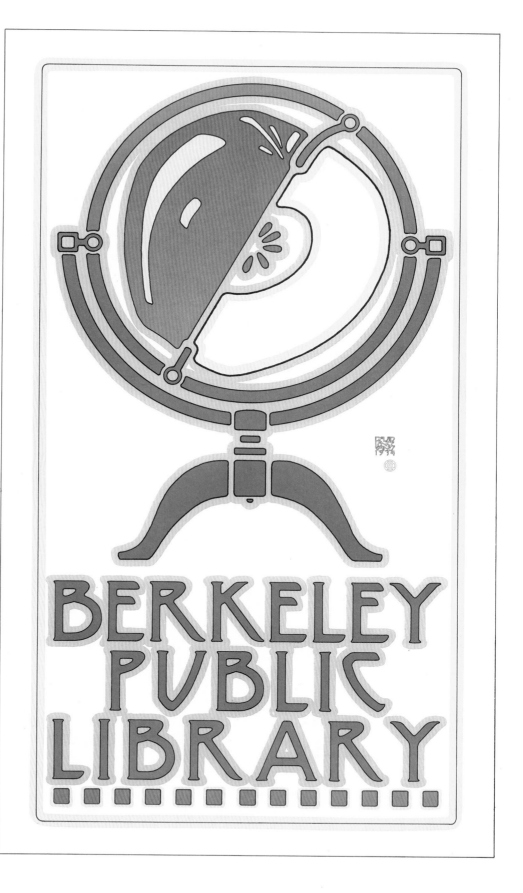

BERKELEY PUBLIC LIBRARY, 1974, FIVE COLORS, 14 x 24'', GOINES 45

WEININGER
BERKELEY CITY COUNCIL

WEININGER, 1975, THREE COLORS, 18 x 24'', GOINES 46

MUSIC AND THE MOVIES, 1975, SEVEN COLORS, 10 x 24", GOINES 47

HOFFMAN BIRTH ANNOUNCEMENT, 1975, FOUR COLORS, 18 x 24'', GOINES 48

CHEZ PANISSE FOURTH BIRTHDAY, 1975, NINE COLORS, 18 x 24″, GOINES 49

CHAMPAGNE DEUTZ, 1975, SEVEN COLORS, 18 x 24'', GOINES 50

XIV SEMAINE INTERNATIONALE DE LA CRITIQUE FRANCAISE
A SERIES OF SEVEN FILMS FROM THE 1975 CANNES FILM FESTIVAL
PRESENTED BY THE LOS ANGELES INTERNATIONAL FILM EXPOSITION
IN ASSOCIATION WITH THE UCLA FILM ARCHIVE· THE UCLA COMMIT-
TEE ON FINE ARTS PRODUCTIONS· & THE PACIFIC FILM ARCHIVE·

OCT 26-NOV 1   NOV 2-NOV 7
ROYCE HALL   PACIFIC FILM ARCHIVE
LOS ANGELES   U·C·ART MUSEUM
825-2953   642-1413

FILMEX

PANDORA'S BOX, 1975, SEVEN COLORS, 13 x 24'', GOINES 52

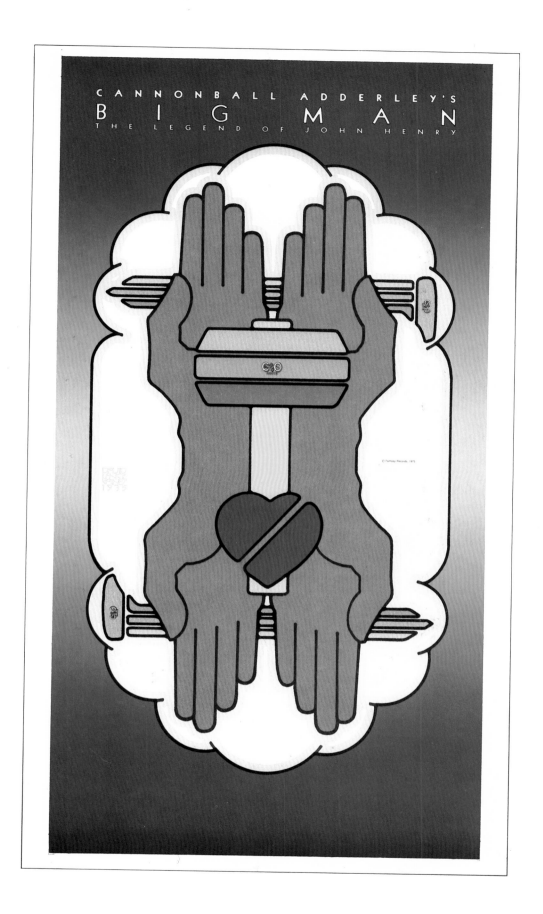

BIG MAN, 1975, ELEVEN COLORS, 14 x 24″, GOINES 53

ANNUNCIATION, 1975, SEVEN COLORS PLUS GOLD, 15 x 24", GOINES 54

SAN FRANCISCO SYMPHONY, 1975, SEVEN COLORS, 15¼ x 24″, GOINES 55

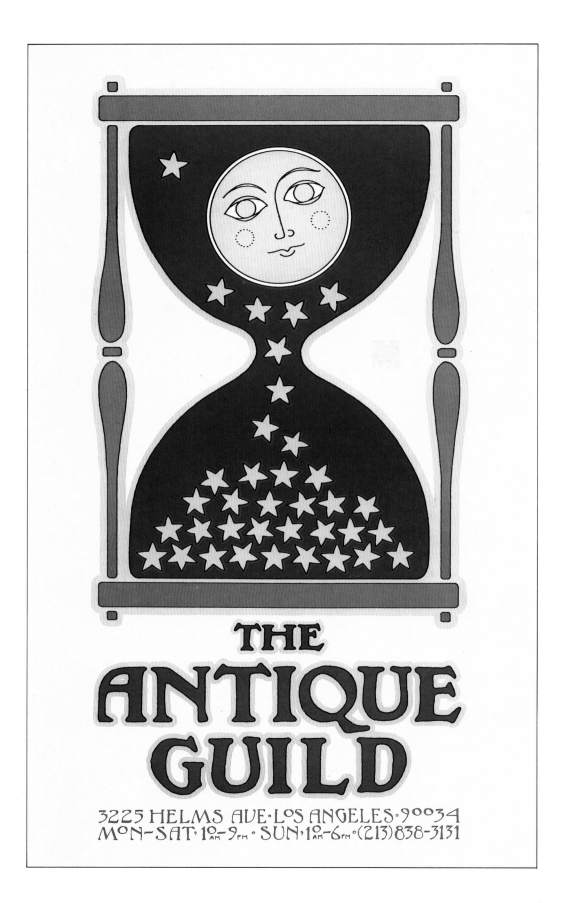

THE ANTIQUE GUILD, 1976, FOUR COLORS, 15 x 24'', GOINES 56

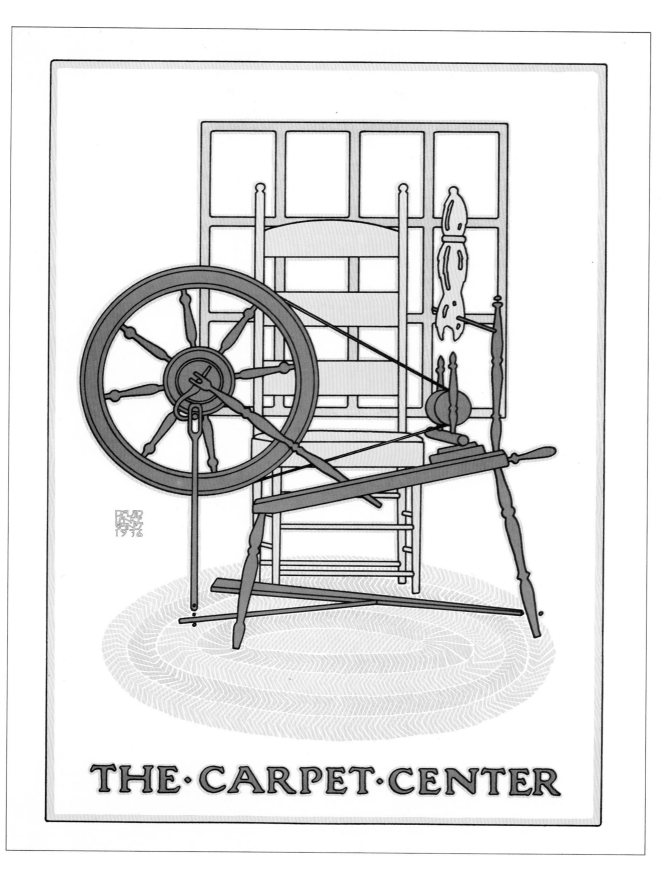

THE CARPET CENTER, 1976, FOUR COLORS, 18 x 24'', GOINES 57

LE MATIN, 1976, SIX COLORS, 16¾ x 24″, GOINES 58

BOOKSHOP·SANTA·CRUZ

1547 PACIFIC GARDEN MALL·SANTA CRUZ·CALIFORNIA·(408) 423-0900

CHEZ PANISSE FIFTH BIRTHDAY, 1976, SEVEN COLORS, 16¼ x 24", GOINES 60

FULL·CIRCLE
FIRST BIRTHDAY·VINTAGE GRAPHICS
1527 FOURTH AVENUE·SEATTLE·WASHINGTON·(206)682-7654

FULL CIRCLE, 1976, FIVE COLORS PLUS GOLD, 18 x 24", GOINES 62

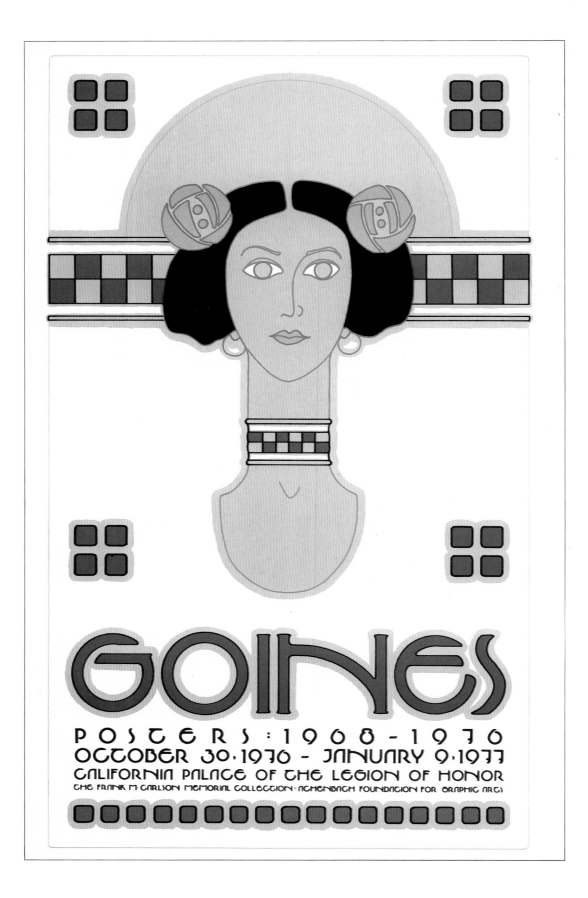

GOINES POSTERS: 1968 –1976, 1976, SIX COLORS, 15 x 24", GOINES 61

QUEEN·OF·HEARTS·BALL

PRESENTED BY COYOTE & MARGO ST·JAMES ♡ AT THE GALLERIA-101 KANSAS ST·S·F·
TO CELEBRATE APRIL FOOLS' DAY·FRIDAY APRIL FIRST·8:30 ᴾᴹ UNTIL 2 ᴬᴹ ♡$10ᵒᵒ PER PERSON
FANTASY COSTUME REQUESTED·COSTUME 'RUNWAY' FASHION SHOW·PALATIAL PRIZES
THREE BANDS ♡♡♡ OBEAH (REGGAE) ♡ THE JOHN GIRTON BAND WITH MARYANN PRICE
♡♡♡♡♡♡♡♡ R·CRUMB & THE CHEAPSUIT SERENADERS ♡♡♡♡♡♡♡♡
♡ADVANCE TICKET SALES ONLY·GET YOUR TICKETS EARLY·ONLY 1500 WILL BE SOLD♡
DIAL: T·E·L·E·T·I·X (BASS) OR CALL COYOTE (415)957-1610 FOR FURTHER INFORMATION♡

MIRAGE, 1977, SIX COLORS, 13½ x 24", GOINES 64

GARLIC

CHEZ·PANISSE GARLIC FESTIVAL
JULY 12·16·1977
1517 SHATTUCK BERKELEY
548·5525

GARLIC, 1977, SEVEN COLORS, 18 x 24", GOINES 65

FAUST, 1977, SEVEN COLORS, 18 x 24'', GOINES 66

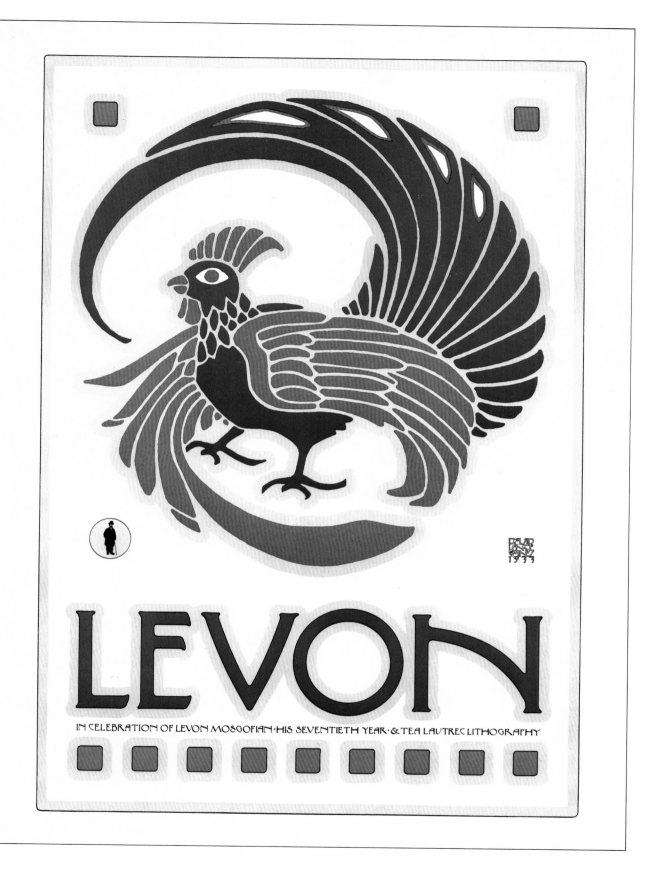

LEVON, 1977, FOUR COLORS, 18 x 24″, GOINES 67

LETTER FROM AN UNKNOWN WOMAN
DIRECTED BY MAX OPHULS(1948)STARRING JOAN FONTAINE & LOUIS JOURDAN
THE PACIFIC FILM ARCHIVE·U·C·ART MUSEUM·2625 DURANT AVE·BERKELEY·CA·
FRIDAY DECEMBER 2·AT 8⁴⁵❖ALSO SHOWING·LE PLAISIR (1951) 7⁰⁰ & 10²⁵·PHONE:642-1412

LETTER FROM AN UNKNOWN WOMAN, 1977, NINE COLORS PLUS GOLD, 18 x 24'', GOINES 68

NOSFERATU

EINE SYMPHONIE DES GRAUENS
DIRECTED BY F·W·MURNAU·1922·STARRING MAX SCHRECK·BASED
ON «DRACULA»·BY BRAM STOKER· 9ª + ALSO THE PHANTOM OF
THE OPERA·1925·7ª·NOVEMBER 2·AT THE PACIFIC FILM ARCHIVE

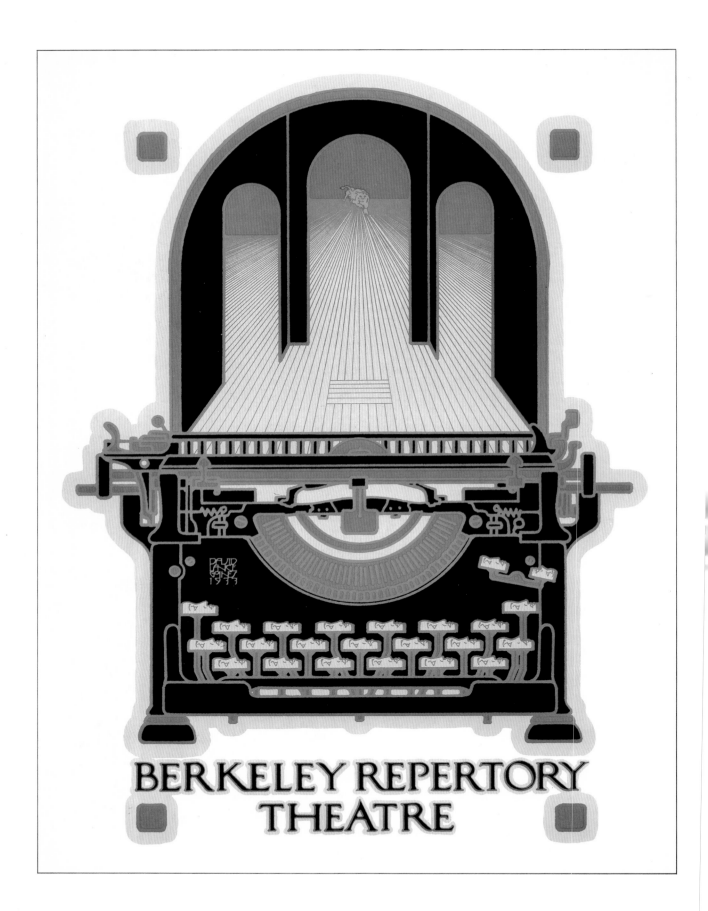

BERKELEY REPERTORY THEATRE, 1977, SIX COLORS, 18 x 24″, GOINES 70

UNIVERSITY ART CENTER, 1978, TEN COLORS, 14¼ x 24″, GOINES 72

NEW YEARS GREETINGS, 1978, SEVEN COLORS PLUS GOLD, 16 x 24", GOINES 71

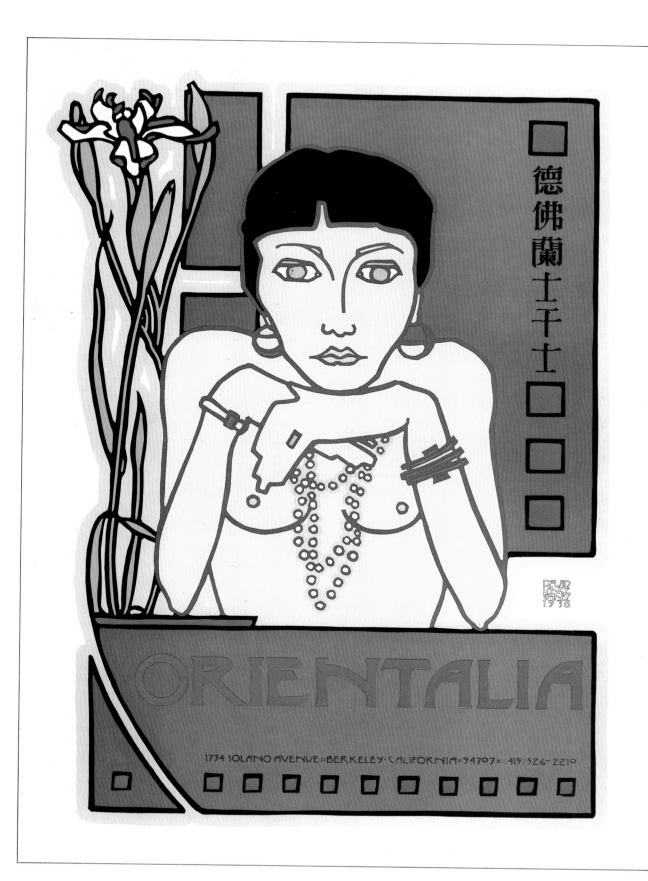

ORIENTALIA, 1978, SEVEN COLORS PLUS GOLD, 18 x 24", GOINES 73

AUGUST, 1978, NINE COLORS, 24 x 18", GOINES 74

CLAUDIA WILKEN AND SARAH LEVERETT ANNOUNCE THE OPENING OF THEIR OFFICES FOR THE
GENERAL PRACTICE OF LAW ON AUGUST FIRST·NINETEEN SEVENTY-EIGHT · WILKEN & LEVERETT·
PLAZA BUILDING·SUITE 700 · 506 FIFTEENTH STREET·OAKLAND·CALIFORNIA·94612·(415) 465-2400

WILKEN & LEVERETT, 1978, SIX COLORS, 16¼ x 24″, GOINES 75

THACKREY & ROBERTSON·SOLE AGENTS FOR DAVID LANCE GOINES SIGNED EDITIONS
2266 UNION STREET·SAN FRANCISCO·CA· 9 4 1 2 3 ·(415)567-4842·CABLE: MEHRLICHT

THACKREY & ROBERTSON, 1978, SEVEN COLORS PLUS GOLD, 14¾ x 24″, GOINES 76

ASILOMAR
TWENTY · EIGHT
SEPTEMBER 22 – 24 · 1978

UNPLEASANT SURPRISES, 1978, NINE COLORS, 15½ x 24", GOINES 78

MESSIAH

CECIL·B·DEMILLE'S KING OF KINGS·1927·WITH·H·B·WARNER· JOSEPH·SCHILDKRAUT·& DOROTHY·CUMMINGS·
THE·PACIFIC·FILM·ARCHIVE·U·C·ART·MUSEUM·FRIDAY·DECEMBER·22·AT·7:30·& SATURDAY·DECEMBER·23·AT·4:30

MESSIAH, 1978, THIRTEEN COLORS, 16⅛ x 24", GOINES 79

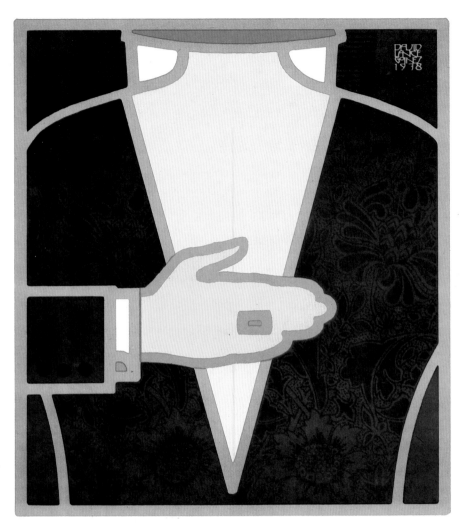

DANCE

THE CINÉ ARTS BALL

SATURDAY·MARCH 24·1979·9 PM ▨▨ UNIVERSITY ART MUSEUM 2626 BANG
ROFT WAY·BERKELEY ▨▨ TICKETS·$12⁵⁰ AVAILABLE AT B·A·S·S··ALL MACY'S·EMR
ORIUM & CAPWELL'S·HINK'S OF BERKELEY·THE PACIFIC FILM ARCHIVE BOX-
OFFICE & THE UNIVERSITY ART MUSEUM COUNCIL ▨▨ TELEPHONE:642-1209

DANCE, 1978, EIGHT COLORS, 16 x 24″, GOINES 80

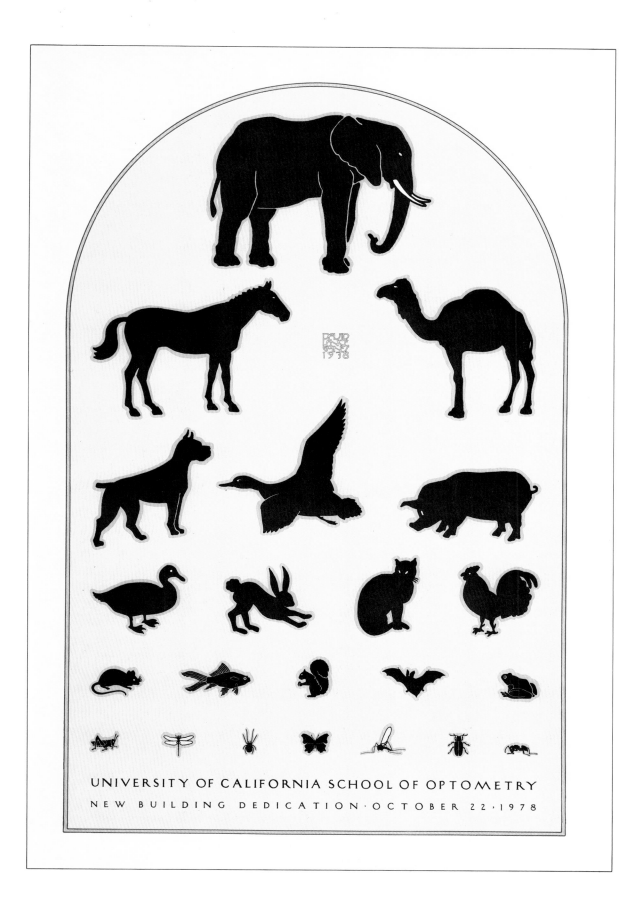

UNIVERSITY OF CALIFORNIA SCHOOL OF OPTOMETRY

NEW BUILDING DEDICATION · OCTOBER 22 · 1978

SCHOOL OF OPTOMETRY, 1979, FOUR COLORS, 16⅝ x 24″, GOINES 81

DOW & FROSINI, 1979, THIRTEEN COLORS, 18 x 24″, GOINES 82

RAVENS

WOOD
WINERY

655 SUTTER STREET, SAN FRANCISCO, CALIFORNIA 94102 (415) 474-2700

RAVENSWOOD, 1979, FIVE COLORS, 16 x 24", GOINES 83

INTERNATIONAL
HOUSE
BERKELEY · CALIFORNIA
1 9 3 0 - 1 9 8 0

INTERNATIONAL HOUSE, 1979, FIVE COLORS PLUS GOLD, 16 x 24", GOINES 84

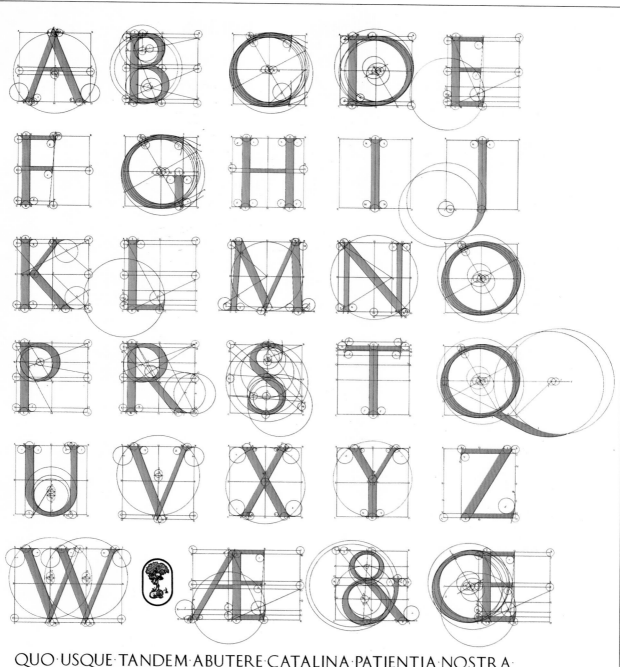

QUO·USQUE·TANDEM·ABUTERE·CATALINA·PATIENTIA·NOSTRA·
QUAM·DIU·ETIAM·FUROR·ISTE·TUUS·NOS·ELUDET·QUEM·AD·FINE
M·SESE·EFFRENATA·JACTABIT·AUDACIA·NIHILNE·TE·NOCTURNUM·
PRÆSIDIUM·PALATI·NIHIL·URBIS·VIGILIÆ·NIHIL·TIMOR·POPULI·NIHIL·
CONCURSUS·BONORUM·OMNIUM·NIHIL·HIC·MUNITISSIMUS·HABEN
DI·SENATUS·LOCUS·NIHIL·HORUM·ORA·VULTUSQUE·MOVERUNT·PA
TERE·TUA·CONSILIA·NON·SENTIS·CONSTRICTAM·JAM·OMNIUM   H
ORUM·SCIENTIA·TENERI·CONJURATIONEM·TUAM·NONKWXYZ&Œ

SECOND DRAFT OF A CONSTRUCTED ROMAN ALPHABET BY DAVID LANCE GOINES BEING A GEOMETRIC ANALYSIS OF THE GREEK & ROMAN CAPITALS & THE ARABIC NUMERALS

A CONSTRUCTED ROMAN ALPHABET, 1979, TWO COLORS, 18 x 24'', GOINES 85

CAFE CHEZ PANISSE, 1980, NINE COLORS, 14⅝ x 24″, GOINES 86

WINGS

DIRECTED BY WILLIAM WELLMAN :: 1928 :: WITH CHARLES ROGERS :: CLARA BOW & RICHARD ARLEN :: ALSO SHOWING · DAWN PATROL · DIRECTED BY HOWARD HAWKS :: 1930 :: WINGS SHOWING AT 4PM & 8PM · DAWN PATROL AT 7PM · JUNE 29TH · 1980 :: AT THE PACIFIC FILM ARCHIVE :: U·C·ART MUSEUM :: PHONE 642-1412

WINGS, 1980, FOUR COLORS, 16¼ x 24″, GOINES 87

MIRAGE EDITIONS, 1980, TEN COLORS, 18 x 24'', GOINES 88

E A T

CHEZ PANISSE NINTH BIRTHDAY AUGUST 28 1980 1330 CAFE & RESTAURANT 1517 SHATTUCK AVENUE BERKELEY CALIFORNIA 94709 548 5525

EAT, 1980, TWELVE COLORS, 16⅞ x 24″, GOINES 89

NORTHFACE

THE NORTH FACE PRODUCES THE FINEST OUTDOOR EQUIPMENT
FOR THE EXPERT AND NOVICE ⊠ PARKAS, SLEEPING BAGS, TENTS,
PACKS & ACCESSORIES ⊠ 1234 FIFTH STREET, BERKELEY, CALIFORNIA
9   4   7   1   0   ⊠   U   S   A

NORTHFACE, 1980, THIRTEEN COLORS, 16⅞ x 24'', GOINES 90

METROPOLIS

DIRECTED BY FRITZ LANG · 1926 · SCRIPT BY THEA VON HARBOU · MAY 19 · 7³⁰ PM · AT THE PACIFIC FILM ARCHIVE · U·C·ART MUSEUM

METROPOLIS, 1981, THIRTEEN COLORS, 18 x 24″, GOINES 91

CHEZ:PANISSE
TENTH · BIRTHDAY

SUNDAY · AUGUST 30TH · 1981 · JOS · PHELPS WINERY
200 TAPLIN ROAD ☙ SAINT HELENA · CALIFORNIA
AT FOUR O'CLOCK ☙ MUSIC · FOOD & WINE ☙ $25 00
ADVANCE RESERVATIONS REQUIRED ☙ 548-5525

CHEZ PANISSE TENTH BIRTHDAY, 1981, FOUR COLORS, 18 x 24", GOINES 92

CARDUCCI & HERMAN LANDSCAPE ARCHITECTS, 1981, SEVEN COLORS, 12¾ x 24″, GOINES 93

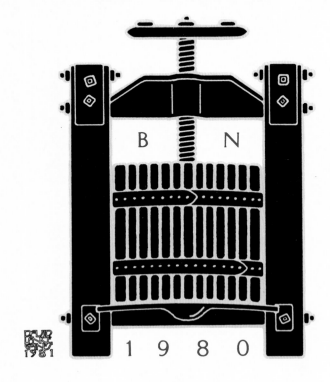

NEYERS

B N

1 9 8 0

NAPA VALLEY
CHARDONNAY

PRODUCED AND BOTTLED BY
NEYERS WINERY
SAINT HELENA, CALIFORNIA

NEYERS, 1981, THREE COLORS, 15¼ x 24″, GOINES 94

CHEZ PANISSE MENU COOKBOOK, 1981, TEN COLORS, 15½ x 24", GOINES 95

QUILT SHOW

 QUILTS ✠ A TRADITION OF VARIATIONS
PRESENTED BY EAST BAY HERITAGE QUILTERS
✠ AT MILLS COLLEGE ART GALLERY ✠
OAKLAND, CALIFORNIA ✠ OCT.9 TO NOV.28,1982

QUILT SHOW, 1982, SEVEN COLORS PLUS BLIND DEBOSSING, 15⅞ x 24″, GOINES 96

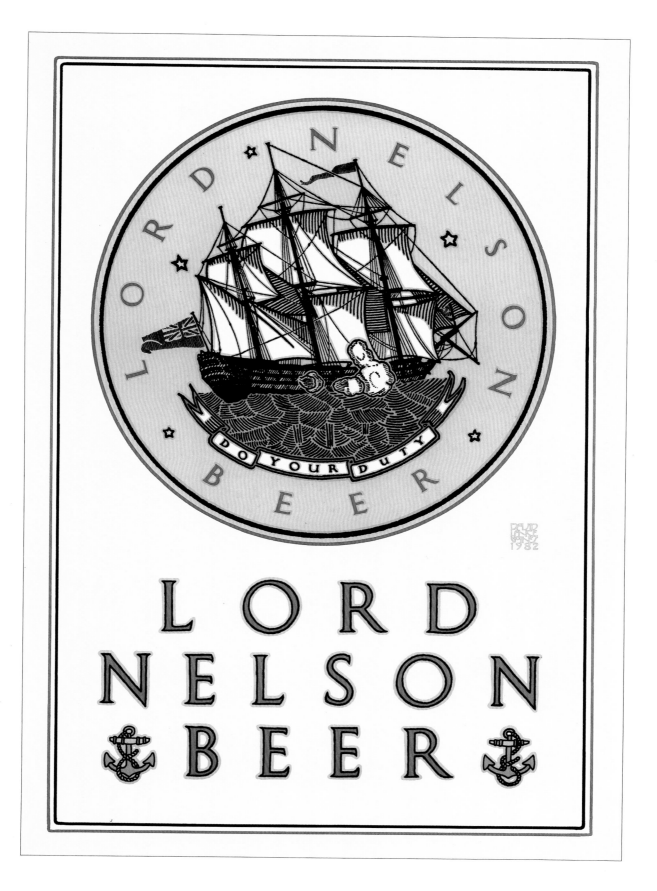

LORD NELSON BEER, 1982, FIVE COLORS, 17 x 24″, GOINES 97

PETER **M** LORRE
DIRECTED·BY FRITZ·LANG
AT·THE·PACIFIC FILM·ARCHIVE
U·C·ART·MUSEUM JULY·22·AT·7³⁰P M

M, 1982, TEN COLORS, 18 x 24″, GOINES 98

DOUBLE SUICIDE, 1982, FOURTEEN COLORS, 17⅝ x 24″, GOINES 99

HUBBARD

KEYBOARD INSTRUMENTS

16TH·17TH & 18TH CENTURY INSTRUMENTS & KITS · 144 MOODY ST··WALTHAM·MA·02154 · TEL:(617) 894·3238

HUBBARD, 1982, THIRTEEN COLORS, 18 x 24″, GOINES 100

CODY'S BOOKS, 1983, TEN COLORS PLUS GOLD, 17½ x 24″, GOINES 101

PARSIFAL, 1983, EIGHT COLORS, 16¾ x 24″, GOINES 102

OAKLAND SYMPHONY, 1983, SIXTEEN COLORS PLUS GOLD, 17⅜ x 24", GOINES 103

T W E L V E

CHEZ·PANI∫∫E TWELFTH BIRTHDAY //⅃ CAFÉ & RE∫TAURANT 1517 ∫HATTUCK
AVENUE · BERKELEY · CALIFORNIA 94709 //⅃/⅃⅂⅃⅂/⅃ 28 AUGU∫T 1983

TWELVE, 1983, TWELVE COLORS, 17¾ x 24", GOINES 104

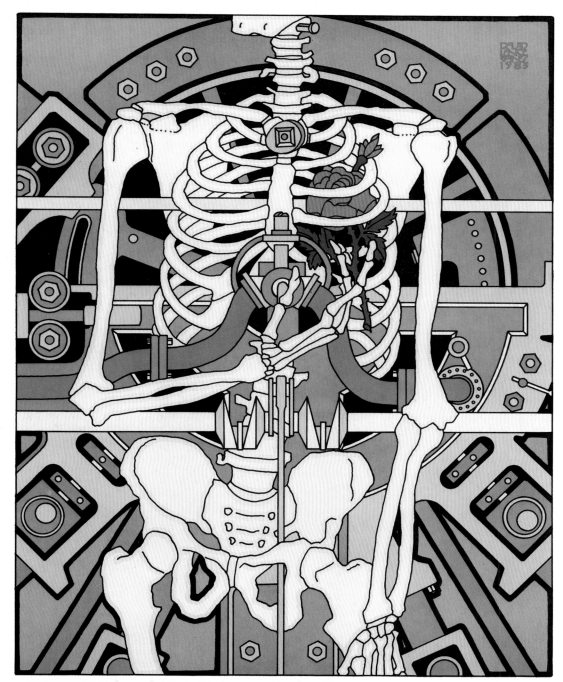

FRANKENSTEIN

FRANKENSTEIN, 1983, ELEVEN COLORS, 17⅛ x 24″, GOINES 107

SHOW, 1983, TEN COLORS PLUS GOLD, 16 x 24", GOINES 105

MANUFACTURER OF MICRO COMPUTERS & PERIPHERALS SINCE 1976

MORROW, 1983, NINE COLORS PLUS GOLD, 16¼ x 24″, GOINES 106

CAROUSEL

ANIMALS

TOBIN FRALEY STUDIOS · CAROUSEL RESTORATION · (415) 654-3031 ⌘ 3246 ETTIE STREET · OAKLAND · CALIFORNIA · 94608

CAROUSEL ANIMALS, 1984, THIRTEEN COLORS, 17¾ x 24", GOINES 108

DOMUS

 THE CARPET CENTER
THIRTY-FIFTH ANNIVERSARY
SEVENTH & PARKER · BERKELEY

DOMUS, 1984, ELEVEN COLORS, 18 x 24″, GOINES 109

KARL KARDEL CO

CONTRACTORS·INTERIOR DESIGN·COLOR
OAKLAND·CALIFORNIA·(415) 261–4149

KARL KARDEL CO., 1984, ELEVEN COLORS, 17⅛ x 24", GOINES 110

THIRTEEN

THIRTEEN, 1984, ELEVEN COLORS, 18 x 24″, GOINES 111

NEW YORK, 1984, NINETEEN COLORS, 16 x 24'', GOINES 112

NORTH FACE

THE NORTH FACE PRODUCES THE FINEST OUTDOOR EQUIPMENT FOR THE EXPERT & NOVICE
CLOTHING · SLEEPING BAGS · TENTS & PACKS 🕮 999 HARRISON STREET · BERKELEY · 94710

NORTH FACE, 1984, TWENTY COLORS, 17⅜ x 24″, GOINES 113

THE POSTER
SANTA BARBARA
817 ANACAPA 93101·(805)965-1319

THE POSTER SANTA BARBARA, 1984, SIXTEEN COLORS, 15³/₁₆ x 24″, GOINES 114

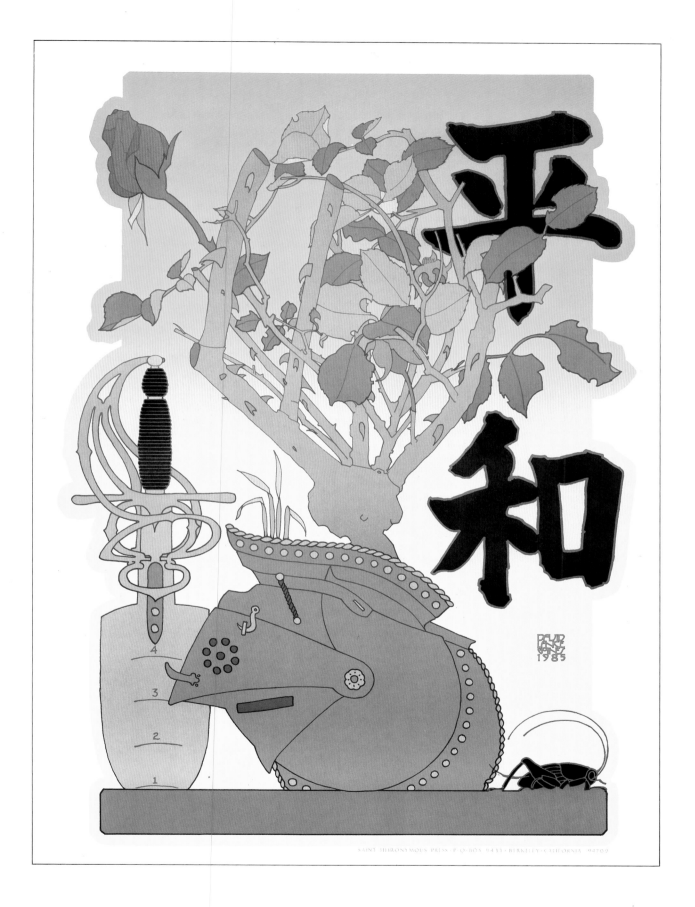

HEIWA, 1985, FOURTEEN COLORS, 17¾ x 24″, GOINES 115

W.A. KING COMPANY, 1985, FOURTEEN COLORS, 16 x 24'', GOINES 116